VANISHED

by Judith Herbst

Lerner Books • London • New York • Minneapolis

First published in the United Kingdom in 2009 by
Lerner Books,
Dalton House,
60 Windsor Avenue,
London SW19 2RR

Website address: www.lernerbooks.co.uk

This edition was updated and edited for UK publication by Discovery Books Ltd.,
First Floor, 2 College Street, Ludlow, Shropshire SY8 1AN

British Library Cataloguing in Publication Data

Herbst, Judith
   Vanished. - 2nd ed. - (The unexplained)
   1. Disappearances (Parapsychology) - Juvenile literature
   I. Title
   001.9'4

ISBN-13: 978 0 7613 4313 4

Printed in Singapore

Table of Contents

'All right,' said the Cheshire Cat; and this time it vanished quite slowly, beginning with the end of the tail, and ending with the grin, which remained some time after the rest of it had gone.

– Lewis Carroll, *Alice's Adventures in Wonderland*

CHAPTER 1
AMELIA AND THE PETROL GAUGE

They called her Lady Lindy, after Charles Lindbergh, the most famous male pilot of the day. She had a broad, gap-toothed grin that made her large eyes dance behind her flying goggles. She wasn't a half-bad pilot – for a girl, that is. Yeah, she held her own, all right. She made the 3,800-kilometre (2,400-mile) run from Hawaii to California and crossed the Atlantic all alone. The Gulf of Mexico too.

By 1937 Amelia Earhart was a world-famous pilot. She had flown across the Atlantic Ocean twice and had completed a 3,800-km (2,400-mile) solo flight across the Pacific Ocean.

She was Amelia Earhart. In the 1930s she was the slickest thing in the skies. So it was very strange that she just disappeared like that. They said that her last message came through at quarter to nine in the morning, 3 July 1937. I was 10 at the time. 'We are on the line of position 157-337.... We are running north and south.' That's what she said. That's all she said.

They searched, of course. Ten ships and 65 planes were out there over the Pacific looking for Lady Lindy. They didn't find a thing. Not one scrap. It was like the clouds swallowed her up. If she'd crashed, there would have been wreckage, don't you think? If she'd been in trouble, she would have radioed a Mayday signal, right? I wonder whatever happened to her.

It has been more than 70 years since Amelia Earhart, together with her navigator, Frederick Noonan, disappeared over the Pacific Ocean. But the mystery of what became of them still intrigues us. Their plan was to circle the globe at the equator – a 46,000-km (29,000-mile) trip no one had ever attempted before.

THE BIG BLUE

The Pacific Ocean is the world's largest and deepest ocean. It's also the world's largest geographical feature, covering one-third of the surface of the Earth. The ocean's 182 million square km (70 million square miles) are dotted with 30,000 islands, most grouped together as the Pacific Islands or Oceania. Some Pacific Islands are no larger than a back garden. In fact, if you subtracted the mass of the largest islands – Hawaii, New Guinea and New Zealand – the remaining thousands put together would only be one quarter the size of the UK.

The Pacific has vast stretches of open ocean and uninhabited islands.

Earhart took off heading east from Oakland, California, USA, flying a Lockheed 10-E Electra, which was fitted with extra-large fuel tanks and radio navigation gear. Her first stop was Miami, Florida. From there she flew out over the Caribbean Sea and on to South America, Africa, India, Myanmar (Burma) and Australia.

Despite insomnia, nausea and severe stomach cramps, Earhart pushed on, logging 35,200 km (22,000 miles) before she set her plane down on a grassy landing strip in Lae, New Guinea, in the South Pacific Ocean. Both Earhart and Noonan were showing signs of exhaustion and the most dangerous part of the trip lay ahead of them.

Only 11,200 km (7,000 miles) of their journey back to California remained. But it was 11,200 km of featureless ocean. Their navigational target was an atoll (a ring-shaped coral island) 2,600 km (1,650 miles)

In San Juan, Puerto Rico, Earhart and Noonan packed their plane for the transatlantic leg of their journey.

GUTS AND LUCK

In the early days of aviation, a pilot needed guts
and a lot of luck. Before electronic instruments, flying
was literally hit or miss. Pilots relied on land features to
guide them to their destinations. They followed railway tracks,
light beacons, roads and rivers. As they drew closer to their
target, they looked for specific markers, such as a church steeple or
a design on a rooftop. If the weather turned bad and visibility
dropped, a pilot could easily become disoriented. Without instruments
and unable to see the horizon line, a pilot had no way of knowing
whether he or she was 'flying right'. This inability to tell up from
down was the main reason that so many planes crashed.

Earhart and Noonan had compasses and some other
instruments, but they were still depending on land features
to help them to reach Hawaii. Over the vast South
Pacific, those features were few and far between.

south-west of Honolulu, Hawaii. Howland Island, with no permanent
inhabitants, is a 2.5 km long speck and a challenge to find even with
modern, sophisticated equipment. For Earhart, Howland was just
barely within range.

>> Final Flight

Earhart and Noonan took off from Lae on the morning of 2 July.
The US Coast Guard ship *Itasca* waited offshore of Howland in
case Earhart needed help locating the island. Earhart esti-
mated that she would arrive at Howland in 24 hours.

N

NORTH AMERICA

Oakland, USA

ATLANTIC OCEAN

Hawaiian Islands

Miami, USA

San Juan, Puerto Rico

Caripito, Venezuela

Dakar, Senegal

PACIFIC OCEAN

equator

SOUTH AMERICA

Natal, Brazil

Earhart and Noonan (pictured on page 11) set out from California, on 21 May 1937. They headed south towards the equator, tracing a route across Florida, Puerto Rico and northern South America. From Natal, Brazil, they crossed over to Senegal, Africa, and continued across the continent. From Africa, Earhart and Noonan flew over the Arabian Sea to Pakistan, India, South-east Asia, Indonesia and Australia. The last leg of their journey was the

most difficult. *After Lae, New Guinea, Earhart and Noonan faced 4,180 km (2,600 miles) of featureless Pacific Ocean before reaching their next target, tiny Howland Island, near Honolulu, Hawaii. Noonan prepared to navigate half the journey in the dark, since they'd be flying at night. Meanwhile, near Howland Island, US navy ships lit all their lights, to serve as markers. The* Itasca *also sent up a plume of black smoke, visible from the plane's altitude.*

Twenty hours into the flight, Earhart established radio contact with *Itasca.* A little while later, she radioed back to ask for a compass heading. *Itasca* heard nothing for about an hour and then, 'We must be on you, *Itasca,* but cannot see you. Fuel is running low. We have been unable to reach you by radio.'

The *Itasca* operator responded, but he did not receive any acknowledgement. After about 15 minutes, Earhart again radioed to ask for a heading. The *Itasca* responded but then heard nothing until 8.44 am, local time. It turned out to be Earhart's last transmission. She was less than 3,600 km (2,250 miles) from Hawaii.

What happened to Amelia Earhart?

The *Baltimore Evening Sun* reported that Earhart may have radioed for help after the plane disappeared. Such reports helped to fuel the hope that she and Noonan would be found alive.

Some people suggested that she had actually been on a secret mission for the government. Instead of heading east when she left New Guinea, she flew north towards the Caroline Islands (modern Palau and Micronesia). As Earhart and Noonan approached Saipan, one of the Mariana Islands, the Electra was shot down by Japanese soldiers patrolling the islands. Earhart and Noonan were taken prisoner and executed. Others thought she and Noonan had landed on a romantic tropical isle and were frolicking on the warm sand, glad to be rid of the pressures of civilized life. Once people started sighting UFOs, they naturally blamed the aliens for Earhart's disappearance. The most likely scenario, though, had Earhart running out of fuel and crashing into the Pacific. Despite an extensive search that began within hours of Earhart's last communication, neither bodies nor wreckage were ever found.

≫ Gone without a Trace?

The years pass. It's now four decades later, and Ric Gillespie of the International Group for Historic Aircraft Recovery (TIGHAR) is working on his own rather intriguing theory. Earhart and Noonan were certainly low on fuel, he says, but they had just enough to set their plane down on a coral reef close to the South Pacific island of Nikumaroro. They made their way to the uninhabited atoll, where they eventually died of starvation and exposure.

Gillespie has made four trips to Nikumaroro in his search for clues, but what he has found so far is less than convincing. He has fragments of a woman's shoe and a sheet of aluminium from a plane.

However, the rivet pattern on the aluminium does not match the Electra's. A couple of years after Earhart's disappearance,

Earhart is shown testing her plane's life raft before packing it on board. If the plane went down in the ocean, Earhart and Noonan could have escaped the wreckage on the raft.

Nikumaroro is an atoll. Even if Earhart and Noonan reached Nikumaroro, they had no fresh water or food and no shelter from the blazing sun.

explorers supposedly discovered bones on the island. But the bones are long gone. Still, Gillespie is confident that he is right.

Elgen Long begs to differ. Long has spent more than two decades piecing together Earhart's flight path and believes Earhart's plane ran out of fuel and plunged into the Pacific. It is resting, he says, 55 km (35 miles) west-northwest of Howland Island, in a cold, watery grave, 5,100 metres down.

An eerie, bleached skeleton of Amelia would not, however, be sitting in the flooded cockpit. The salty Pacific Ocean would have long ago dissolved her mortal remains. However, the Electra's aluminium fuselage would probably be resting on the bottom, parked in its final hangar, patiently waiting for the tourists to arrive.

CHRIS AND THE TRIANGLE

If you ask me, I don't think the admiral knew where he was going half the time. I was on the Pinta *with 26 other men when we sailed from Palos on the Spanish coast to what I found out later were the Canary Islands, off the coast of West Africa. The admiral thought we'd reached China. See what I mean?*

After that, we headed west. We caught the trade winds and made pretty good progress, averaging about 225 km (140 miles) a day. Of course, there wasn't an awful lot to see because by then we were on open ocean, bound for either glory or disaster – take your pick.

We were somewhere in the North Atlantic, I think, when we started to come into some really thick seaweed. Let me tell you, it was nasty. The admiral – if you can believe it – was practically doing a jig on the deck. 'We're almost there, boys!' he cried. 'Seaweed's a sign that we're close to land.' Then the wind died down and it didn't look like it was going to rain any time soon, so we sat there, not exactly feeling confident.

Even though the admiral kept telling us not to worry, any fool could see we were in trouble. The current was carrying us in a strange clockwise direction and the ship's compass had started to go haywire. When we complained to the admiral, he just waved us off. 'A compass never points to true north,' he said. 'It's always a little off.' Of course, we all thought, rolling our eyes. And Queen Isabella is really a mermaid.

The *Pinta*, the *Niña* and the *Santa Maria (facing page)* first set sail across the Atlantic Ocean from Spain in 1492. The ships were guided by Christopher Columbus (*left*), an Italian navigator who was looking for a route to Asia.

I'll tell you what I think. I think good old Admiral Where-in-the-world-am-I? had blundered into some kind of haunted sea – not that it bothered him. He's talking about coming back here again next year. You'd think I'd be scared to sail with him, but I'm not. Like I said, the man has an awful sense of direction. We'll probably end up in Egypt.

Sailing west from the Canary Islands, Columbus could hardly avoid the region that would one day be called the Sargasso Sea. It is a vast, slow-flowing field of brown gulfweed, roughly the size of the United States of America. Here, the weather is almost diabolically calm, and the surrounding currents create a lazy whirlpool, like a pan of soup just coming to a boil. It is hot, dry and windless, a place where a ship

THE HORSE LATITUDES

Sailing with the wind was tricky and dangerous, an adventure that could scare you as well as stir your spirit. As long as a steady wind filled the sails, a ship made good progress, but when the wind died, the sea could hold a ship hostage for days on end as food and water slowly dwindled away.

Sailors quickly learned to be wary of two weather belts that girdle the Earth near the latitudes of 30°N and 30°S. The subtropic oceans under these weather belts are often very calm, with light winds. The belts became known as the horse latitudes because, according to legend, Spanish sailors transporting horses to the New World often had to resort to throwing the horses overboard to conserve water.

Stories of hideous sea creatures abounded in European exploration. Sailors were nervous about travelling unknown waters and large, unfamiliar fish easily became 'monsters'.

might drift for days, her sails as limp as bed sheets, her hull creaking for want of a rescuing breeze.

To Columbus' crew, the Sargasso Sea was unfamiliar and frightening. But while Columbus himself was carefully recording the facts in his ship's logbook, his men were doing just the opposite. Fueled by superstition and an I-bet-you-can't-top-this mentality, the sailors thought up quite a tale for the folks back home. By the time they reached Portugal, the seaweed had become a sinister life form that crawled up and over the rails and lashed sailors to the masts. Instead of dolphins and tuna, horrible sea serpents rose from the darkened depths. Fire poured from the sky and a bubbling whirlpool threatened to spin the three ships to a watery death. Compass needles turned crazily in the magnetic vacuum and . . .

Hey, wait a minute! This sounds a lot like a prototype for the Bermuda Triangle!

And indeed, that is exactly what it is. Over five centuries later, there are aliens instead of sea serpents and a vortex instead of a whirlpool. The seaweed is no longer mentioned and when fire rains from the sky, it's known as a meteor shower. However, the magnetic vacuum is still

ATLANTIC OCEAN

BERMUDA

FLORIDA

BAHAMAS

CUBA

HAITI

DOMINICAN REPUBLIC

PUERTO RICO

The Bermuda Triangle originally traced its shape from Florida to Puerto Rico to Bermuda. It expanded to include much of the east coast of the US and the central Atlantic Ocean.

there, sucking up sailing ships, fishing boats, Beechcraft planes, DC-3s and fighter jets with equal relish.

The first modern Bermuda Triangle stretched from the tip of Florida to Bermuda to Puerto Rico. However, when Flight 19 was lost in 1945, just north of the Triangle, a Bermuda Square had to be drawn to include it. A Bermuda Trapezoid was needed to account for the disappearance of the *Star Tiger* in 1948. The latest Bermuda 'Triangle' is a big five-sided shape that takes in the entire East Coast of the US, all the way down to South America and east to the Azores. The Azores were added to include the *Mary Celeste,* one of the mysteriess that keeps the myth of the Bermuda Triangle stuck together.

FLIGHT 19

Almost every Bermuda Triangle book opens with the 'mystery' of Flight 19. Five navy bomber planes flying in formation suddenly vanished on a routine training mission in 1945. How could five experienced pilots just disappear? Well, the pilots were actually trainees following a flight leader whose compass had failed. The sea was rough and fuel was running low. Add it up, and you get a tragic, but not very mysterious, disappearance.

≫ The Mystery of the *Mary Celeste*

The story of the *Mary Celeste* is a true mystery. It is, in fact, one of a handful of disappearances that remain unexplained. (Nearly all the others have been attributed to bad weather, engine or structural failure, pilot error or, in one case, a possible hijacking.)

The *Mary Celeste* had sailed for Genoa, Italy, from New York City in November 1872. Her captain was Benjamin Briggs, and he took with him his wife, his young daughter and a crew of eight. On 4 December 1872, another ship, the *Dei Gratia,* found the *Mary Celeste* abandoned and drifting, nearly 950 km (600 miles) west of Gibraltar.

Nothing seemed amiss on board the two-masted ship. The cargo was intact and the galley was shipshape,

The *Mary Celeste* was a type of two-masted sailing ship called a half-brigantine. Half-brigs were often used as merchant ships, carrying cargo from a seller to a buyer.

with six months' worth of untouched provisions. The sails were torn but still quite serviceable. The ship's logbook lay where the captain had left it, his final entry noting that they had passed the Azores on 24 November. Only two things were missing (aside from the 11 people, of course): the ship's official papers and the lifeboat.

At first, the solution to the mystery seems ridiculously obvious. Everybody piled into the lifeboat and rowed away. But why would 11 people forsake a perfectly seaworthy ship for a cramped rowing boat 160 km (100 miles) from land?

Suspicion immediately fell upon the captain and crew of the *Dei Gratia.* They were accused of storming the *Mary Celeste* and killing everyone on board so they could take the ship for the salvage money it would bring. However, a court of inquiry could find no evidence and the captain was cleared.

It was then suggested that the *Dei Gratia's* owner had conspired with the *Mary Celeste's* crew to kill Captain Briggs and his family and sink the ship so that he could collect the insurance money. However, the crew botched the job, and everybody ended up getting killed. This theory, however, raised more questions than it tried to answer, so it too, was dismissed.

With so few clues, people had a free-for-all guessing what might have happened on board the *Mary Celeste.* Everything from waterspouts to a stranding on a 'ghost island' – a shifting sandbar that forms and reforms – was suggested. Some thought that food poisoning might have driven a hallucinating crew to jump overboard. Others pointed to the only hatch found open and suggested that alcohol fumes had blown the cover off. (The *Mary Celeste* was carrying 1,700 barrels of commercial alcohol.) Then the captain, seeing a smoky vapour pour from the hold, feared that the ship was about to catch fire and ordered everyone into the lifeboat. All we have – and are ever likely to have – are bits and pieces of theories, none of which fit together. The mystery remains and this is why the *Mary Celeste* is so beloved by those who believe the Bermuda Triangle is somehow cursed.

≫ Natural or Supernatural?

It's certainly true that ships have gone down in these waters, never to be seen again. Planes have vanished without a trace. Fishing boats and pleasure craft have disappeared. But were strange, supernatural forces responsible? Did aliens in secret underwater outposts suck down all these vessels? Not quite.

It is a fact of life that pilots make errors of judgement. They become disoriented in bad weather. Engines fail. Ships run aground or hit icebergs.

Vincent Gaddis could be considered the creator of the Bermuda Triangle. In his 1965 book, *Invisible Horizons*, Gaddis suggested an explanation for all the Triangle's mysterious vanishings. The US Navy, he wrote, was conducting something called the Philadelphia Experiment, trying to eliminate the Earth's magnetic field. The resulting vortex would suck down ships and planes (*left*) in sensitive spots around the world. Can you guess what the navy thought of Gaddis' theory?

They capsize and sink in fierce, unexpected storms. Explosions happen. Hijackings occur. Crews mutiny. Even in this ultra-modern world of ours, pirates still roam the seas. And the seas are vast. They are deep. If a rescue team is not quickly dispatched, wreckage will sink without a trace. Bodies will be lost forever.

But planes don't just fall out of the sky!

Yes, sadly, they do and the ocean claims them remarkably fast.

It seems that the haunted sea we all love to fear is more myth than curse, more fake than fact. However, some legends just won't sink.

Dan's Daring Disappearance

I have never been so scared in my life. The man was sitting right next to me! I remember. He was in seat 18C. We had just started going down the runway and I was thinking about how take-offs and landings are the most dangerous part of the flight. That was odd, now that I think of it.

The flight attendant comes down the aisle, checking to make sure every-body's wearing their seatbelt. The guy hands her a note. He's wearing sunglasses and a dark suit and he doesn't look menacing or anything. He's just a passenger on his way to Seattle, like the rest of us. Only he isn't.

The note says that he's got a bomb and he's going to blow up the plane if he doesn't get $200,000 in cash and four parachutes when we land.

Well, the flight attendant is cool and doesn't say anything, but when we reach Seattle, they give the guy what he wants, and he lets everybody go, except the pilot and some of the crew. Then they take off again.

Now, this you won't believe. The guy orders the pilot to fly to Mexico, but long before they get there, he somehow gets the cabin door open, straps on a parachute and jumps! They're 10,000 feet up, the winds are gusting at 80 knots and it's freezing, but the guy jumps! With the money!

They never found him.

The Northwest Airlines plane *(facing page)* hijacked by D B Cooper sits on the runway in Seattle, Washington, USA, as it is refuelled. Cooper seemed ill-equipped to skydive out of a jet in high winds *(below)*.

The Northwest Airlines crew recounts the hijacking at a press conference. Cooper first passed a threatening note to the flight attendant (*above, right*), then warned her that he was carrying a bomb.

That was only the beginning, although most people thought it was the end. No one, the federal agents said, could have survived a jump over rugged wilderness terrain in such dreadful weather conditions – especially a man in a business suit! He had called himself Dan Cooper when he purchased his Northwest Airlines flight ticket in Portland, Oregon, on 24 November 1971. Whoever he was, the Federal Bureau of Investigation (FBI) said, he was probably dead now.

But the whole thing was deeply unsettling. Cooper had, in fact, hijacked a Boeing 727 and exited the plane with $200,000 in $20 bills. The stunt was beyond risky. It was insane. However, Cooper did have a parachute – four of them, in fact – and nobody knew anything about him. Had he ever jumped before? Had he, perhaps, been a paratrooper? Did he have more of a plan than authorities supposed? Was it possible that he could have survived? The FBI were worried. It was a very creepy thought.

Months became years, and Cooper started to become something of a folk hero to people in the north-west. They wrote songs about him, celebrating his reckless deed and what some people thought was his success in eluding the FBI. Not the slightest hint of Dan Cooper – either alive or dead – ever surfaced. Then, in 1980, an eight-year-old boy found a muddy packet of money while walking on the banks of the Columbia River near Portland, Oregon.

COOPER CASH

Children find a lot of interesting things when they're out exploring. Stones, arrowheads, watches. Sometimes they even find money – small change and, if they're lucky banknotes. But when Brian Ingram found bundles of $20 bills on a muddy river bank, he knew the money hadn't just fallen out of the sky. Or had it? Brian and his family turned the money over to the police and later learned his find was part of the Cooper ransom. Brian received a $2,760 reward.

In February 1980, eight-year-old Brian Ingram found $5,800 along the banks of the Columbia River. Here he shows reporters where he discovered the money – still in bank bundles.

Federal investigators examined the damaged $20 bills found on the banks of the Columbia River. Some thought it indicated that Cooper had first landed at that spot, but others argued that the river current could have carried the money there.

When the money's serial numbers were checked, they were found to match some of those from the bills given to Cooper. However, most of the money – along with the wheat-coloured bank bag in which it had been placed – was missing. After almost a decade, the plot was beginning to thicken.

>> Duane and the Missing Years

In 1995 Duane Weber lay dying in a hospital in Florida. His wife, Jo, was at his side. They had been married for 17 years, which had been good ones, mostly. Duane had walked into Jo's life in the late 1970s and Jo had fallen for him, even though Duane had some secrets. But there, on the thick hospital bed with the stiff, white sheets, Duane Weber was about to share one of them.

'Jo', he whispered. 'Listen. I'm Dan Cooper.'

Jo blinked. 'What?' she said. 'What do you mean?' She had never heard the name and had no idea what her husband was talking about. Her face was blank.

Weber searched his wife's eyes and then, frustrated, cried out, 'Oh, let it die with me!' But it didn't.

Two months after Duane passed away, Jo sold his van. When the new owners were cleaning it out, they came upon a wallet. It contained US Navy discharge papers for bad conduct in Duane's name. It also held a Social Security card and a Missouri State Penitentiary (prison) release form for someone named John C Collins. Jo was very curious.

Some time later, during a conversation with a friend about Duane's mysterious past, Jo mentioned that her husband had admitted injuring his knee in a parachuting accident.

'What!'

'Yes, just before he died, he told me he had jumped out of a plane and hurt his knee.'

Jo's friend gasped. Did Jo ever wonder, she asked, if Duane might have been D B Cooper?

'Who?'

When D B Cooper hijacked an aeroplane, he broke the law under the Air Piracy Act of 1961 (Cooper's FBI wanted poster is shown, left). That is, he broke a law enacted by the US Congress. The government does not take air piracy lightly and hijackers are pursued by the Federal Aviation Administration (FAA), the Department of Defense (DOD) and the FBI. After Cooper escaped, the FBI launched an exhaustive search, including sending Identification Orders (wanted posters) to police agencies across the country. Cooper's hijacking also prompted the FAA to institute a procedure that's become a familiar routine in any airport – the screening of all passengers and their carry-on luggage.

'The skyjacker! The man who jumped out of a plane in the early 1970s with a bag of money and was never found!'

In May 1996, Jo Weber was in the library, poring over a book about the infamous D B Cooper. The FBI's composite sketch looked eerily like a younger Duane and the description matched: 1.85 m tall, 75 kg, black hair, mid-40s, a chain-smoker. Then, Jo remembered, there was that dream. One night, Duane had mumbled something in his sleep about leaving his fingerprints on the aft stairs. He had woken up in a sweat.

Aft stairs? Jo had thought at the time. Like on an aeroplane?

Jo read on. The wheat-coloured canvas bag! She had seen that! It had been in a cool box in Duane's van. And there was a plane ticket for a flight on Northwest – it had been mixed in with some old tax records.

The whole thing seemed impossible. Who had she married? D B Cooper, Duane Weber or John Collins? One was dishonorably discharged from the navy, one had been in prison and one was an airline hijacker. One or all of these men had died in a Florida hospital, known to his friends as a mild-mannered antiques dealer.

If Jo's husband had, indeed, been D B Cooper, he had pulled off quite a disappearance. On that night in 1971, he had leaped into infamy and vanished without a trace. He had scared everyone but injured no one. He had got away with the money but had spent almost none of it.

It was death that finally found him and Cooper had no choice but to confess. Death knew his real name.

CHAPTER 4

Prison Break

They said we were the worst of the worst, and that's why we wound up on the Rock. Al Capone was there, and so was Machine Gun Kelly. The Choctaw Kid was in for 99 years plus life. Gangsters, racketeers, murderers, train robbers. Bad guys, all of us. That's what they said.

The place was awful. Foghorns all the time, bellowing in the middle of the night like trapped animals, like us, howling to be set free. It was damp, cold and damp and I swear, I never saw so many pelicans. That's how this hole got its name. A Spanish explorer once called it the Isla de los Alcatraces. The island of pelicans. Alcatraz.

They told us we'd never be able to escape. If the freezing water didn't get us, the sharks would. A few men tried anyway. They didn't make it. Then came Frank Morris. On the day he arrived, he said he was leaving. He'd be the one. Took him six months to set it up, and then one night he was gone. To this day, nobody knows what happened to him.

Frank had probably drowned, they said. They never found his body, but they couldn't leave it that way. They couldn't have people thinking that somebody might have actually escaped from the escape-proof prison. So a little while later, they shut the place down for good.

I hear they're giving tours these days. Frank would have thought that was funny. Maybe he's laughing right now.

Frank Morris was a bank robber and had served time in prisons here and there. However, he had a fondness for escaping, so after his last attempt, they sentenced him to 10 years and sent him to Alcatraz.

Alcatraz Penitentiary (facing page) was large, cold and impersonal. It was built to house convicts who had tried to escape other prisons, as Frank

Morris looked at the cold rock walls and heard the shuffle of dead men's feet. He heard the clang of iron doors meeting locks that couldn't be picked. He smelled the pungent disinfectant. No, he thought, this isn't for me. By the end of his first day on the Rock, he had already started to plan his escape.

≫ The Plan Is Hatched

Alcatraz sits upon a tiny, wind-blown island in San Francisco Bay, California, USA, a mere 1.6 km (1 mile) from Fishermen's Wharf and the tourists who pay to look at the famous prison through telescopes.

Alcatraz sits on an island in the middle of San Francisco Bay, California, USA. Before it was a prison, Alcatraz was a military post, guarding the entrance to the bay.

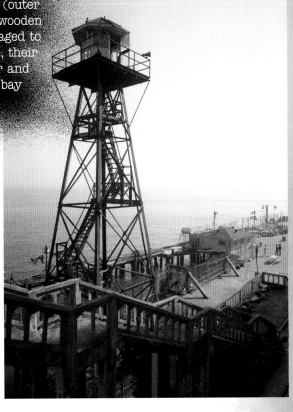

Guards watched the perimeter (outer edge) of Alcatraz Island from wooden towers. Even if prisoners managed to get past the guards and fences, their chances of surviving the water and the dangerous currents of the bay were slim.

There were guards, of course, and fences strung with barbed wire. During the day, a prisoner had little chance to get to the water's edge without being seen. Even if he made it, he had nowhere to go except into the icy waters of San Francisco Bay, where hungry sharks and dangerous currents challenged him to take his best shot. The lights on the shore across the bay shone gaily. The hilly, sun-soaked streets were so tantalizingly close but impossible to reach – if, thought Morris, you were stupid enough to try to swim, which Morris wasn't. He already knew how he was going to get off the island. He just needed to find a way out of the prison.

Within weeks of his arrival, Morris learned that three years earlier, a fan motor had been removed from a ventilation shaft leading to the roof above his cell block. The motor had never been replaced. That meant the shaft should be open all the way up to the roof. It was the perfect escape route. How would Morris get into the shaft? It seemed impossible, unless . . .

Just beneath Morris' sink was an air vent. Beyond the vent, a narrow corridor for water pipes and cables ran along the outer wall. If Morris could enlarge the hole so he could crawl into the corridor, he could make his way to the shaft. Then he could get up onto the roof and be gone!

HARD TIME

At Alcatraz, every day was ruled by the prison routine. Bells and whistles told inmates when to wake up, when to eat, when to take a break from their prison jobs and when to get back to work. Coming or going, inmates waited through head counts and cutlery counts and trudged through metal detectors. At night, after lights-out, inmates had nothing to do but listen to ships' foghorns wail. Escape was unceasingly tempting.

He'd need tools, which were easy enough to steal from the prison workshop. He would also have to hide what he was doing. One of the inmates had an accordion, and that gave him an idea. He could order one for himself, paying for it with money that he had earned in the workshop. Then he could lean the accordion against the hole. As the work progressed and the hole grew larger, Morris realized he'd have to make a false section of wall. He also decided that his escape plan – now almost fully hatched – had a better chance of success if he had some accomplices.

>> Papier Mâché Heads and Water Wings

John and Clarence Anglin had turned bank robbing into a family enterprise. And thanks to the California prison system, they were still spending Sunday dinner times

Clarence Anglin *(left)* and John William Anglin *(right)* were sent to Alcatraz after several attempts to escape from prison in Georgia, USA.

together. (They were held, of course, in different cells.) Toughened by frequent stays in the state penitentiary, the Anglins would make clever breakout companions. Morris eagerly recruited them.

They would make their escape in the dead of night, Morris told them, leaving behind papier mâché heads on their pillows and fake bodies under the covers.

'How do we get across the bay?' the Anglins wanted to know.

'Water wings', Morris told them. 'Or maybe a raft. We inflate plastic rain-coat sleeves with air. The coats are right there in the basement workshop.'

'Hey! We could steal a new one each day!' said Clarence, grinning.

'Yeah! And wear it back to our cells!'

Clearly, the Anglins liked this idea.

'It'll take some time', Morris said.

'We got nothing but time', said Clarence.

Morris had served less than a year of his sentence when the digging was complete, the papier mâché heads were painted and dry,and the way to the roof was clear.

'Let's go', said the Anglins eagerly. 'Let's go tonight.'

But Morris wanted to wait. 'I need to study the currents first', he told them.

'What for?'

'Do you know how cold that water is?'

The Anglins shrugged. It was a detail they didn't think was too important.

'Cold', said Morris. 'Cold enough to kill you. Are you in the mood to fight a current and maybe end up working against it while the water's freezing your legs off until you can't feel them anymore and you can't kick? When you're moving with the current, it takes less time.'

So the Anglins agreed to wait. But their patience quickly wore thin, and some time around nine o'clock on the evening of 11 June Morris heard John Anglin's muffled voice on the other side of the fake wall.

'We're going', he hissed.

'No', Morris whispered back. It was a week before the agreed-upon date. 'Yes. Now', said Anglin and a moment later he was working his way along the utility corridor towards the ventilation shaft.

THE MORRIS-ANGLIN ESCAPE ROUTE

N

ESCAPE ROUTE

POWERHOUSE

San Francisco Bay

ALCATRAZ

WATER TOWER

RECREATION YARD

MODEL TOWER

Soon after lights-out at 9.30 pm on the night of 11 June 1962, Morris and the Anglins began their escape. They crawled out of their cells through the tunnels they had spent months digging. They then made their way down a utility corridor and climbed up a shaft to the cell house roof. Dodging the sweeping beams of the prison searchlights, they ran across the rooftop and

OFFICERS'
RESIDENCES

CELL
HOUSE

LIGHTHOUSE

climbed down some pipes along an exterior wall. Once on the ground, they ran for the shelter of the powerhouse, a large building which housed the prison's generators. From there, the three escapees climbed over two fences and headed for the water's edge.

Morris had no choice. When the lights were turned off for the night, he set the papier mâché head on his pillow, shaped the blankets into a vague human form and crawled into the utility corridor. Within minutes he had joined John and Clarence Anglin on the roof of the prison. Dodging the powerful lights on top of the guardhouses, the three men slipped to the ground. The entire island was bathed by floodlights. Searching out the few shadows, the men moved to the inner chain-link fence, scaled it and then tackled the barbed-wire fence that marked the outer perimeter. Stealthily, they crept to the water's edge, inflated their makeshift water wings and entered the icy, black waters of San Francisco Bay.

≫ Gone!

Nobody knew there had been a prison break until the following morning. By then Morris and the Anglins were either lying at the bottom of San Francisco Bay or had disappeared in the crowded city they had remarkably managed to reach.

The police, the Coast Guard and prison officials searched the water, of course, but all they found was a plastic bag with some family photographs, a few addresses, and a receipt made out to Clarence Anglin. It was a tantalizing piece of evidence that meant absolutely nothing.

The bay had been calm and the currents in their favour, but no one ever reported seeing the men whose daring escape closed Alcatraz. Had the freezing waters numbed them and pulled them under, one by one? Had they been killed in a shoot-out somewhere, their fingers clutching bank-bags filled with hastily stolen notes? Or did they all laugh softly from a table in a rural restaurant when they learned that National Park Service rangers had started giving tours of the prison you couldn't get out of?

Whatever the outcome, it was quite a disappearance.

≫ Find Out More

Books//

Brelin, Theresa. *Prisoner in Alcatraz* Barrington Stoke Ltd. 2004.

Lee Stone, Tanya. *Amelia Earhart* (DK Biography) Dorling Kindersley, 2007.

Oxlade, Chris. *The Mystery of the Bermuda Triangle* (Can Science Solve...?) Heinemann Library, 2006.

Websites//

Alcatraz National Park
http://www.nps.gov/alcatraz/
On the official Alcatraz website, you can learn more about the history of Alcatraz island and read about the escape attempts made by the inmates.

The Earhart Project
http://www.tighar.org/Projects/Earhart/AEdescr.html
TIGHAR's website features photographs, maps, news stories and myths about Earhart's disappearance and the continuing search for clues to this mystery.

The Un-Mystery of the Bermuda Triangle
http://www.unmuseum.org/triangle.htm
The Unmuseum presents its argument for dismissing the supernatural aspect of the Bermuda Triangle. The website includes a brief history of Bermuda Triangle lore.

>> Index

>> About the Author

Born in Baltimore, Maryland, USA, Judith Herbst grew up in Queens, New York, where she learned to jump double skipping ropes with amazing skill. She has since lost that ability. A former English teacher, she ran away from school to become a writer. Her first book for children was *Sky Above and Worlds Beyond,* whose title, she admits, was much too long. She loves to write and would rather be published, she says, than be rich, which has turned out to be the case. Herbst spends her summers in Maine on a lake with her cats and laptop.

>> Photo Acknowledgements

Photographs and illustrations in this book are used by permission of: © Bill Hauser/Independent Picture Service, pp 4–5, 10–11, 12, 20, 22–23, 27, 31, 39, 42–43, 44–45; © Brown Brothers, p 6; © Stuart Klipper, p 7; © Bettmann/CORBIS, pp 8, 14, 16, 26, 28, 29, 30, 35, 40; © Hulton|Archive by Getty Images, pp 11, 22; © CORBIS, p 13; © Reuters/CORBIS, p 15; Knights of Columbus Headquarters Museum, p 17; © Fortean Picture Library, pp 19, 25; © Time Life Pictures/Getty Images, p 32; courtesy of the Library of Congress, pp 34 (HABS, CAL,38-ALCA,1-A-20), 36 (HABS, CAL,38-ALCA,1-1), 37 (HABS, CAL,38-ALCA,1-I-1), 38 (HABS, CAL,38-ALCA,1-A-23). Cover image by © Bettmann/CORBIS.